LIFT OFF

to
Certificate

Teacher's Book

Cornelsen & OXFORD

LIFT OFF TO CERTIFICATE
Teacher's Book

Das Lehrerhandbuch wurde verfasst von: Isobel Williams

Mock Exam Tasks for The European Language Certificates – Certificate in English (ICC, Frankfurt)

Projektleitung: Helga Holtkamp

Redaktion: Susanne Schütz

Redaktionelle Mitarbeit: Christine House, Andrew Dowdall

Layout/Herstellung: Sabine Theuring

Zu **LIFT OFF TO CERTIFICATE** sind auch erhältlich:

Student's Book   Best.-Nr. 21564
CD   Best.-Nr. 21661

1. Auflage €

5. 4. 3. 2. 1.   Die letzten Ziffern bezeichnen
05 04 03 02 01   Zahl und Jahr des Druckes.

Bestellnummer 21580

© Cornelsen & Oxford University Press GmbH & Co., Berlin 2001

Alle Rechte vorbehalten.

Das Werk und seine Teile sind urheberrechtlich geschützt. Jede Verwertung in anderen als den gesetzlich zugelassenen Fällen bedarf deshalb der vorherigen schriftlichen Einwilligung des Verlages.

Druck und Weiterverarbeitung: Druckerei zu Altenburg

ISBN 3-8109-2158-0

Vertrieb: Cornelsen Verlag

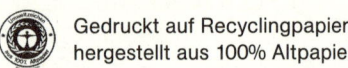
Gedruckt auf Recyclingpapier, hergestellt aus 100% Altpapier.

Inhaltsverzeichnis

Unit		Page
	Introduction	3
1	Hello, nice to meet you	5
2	Hobbies and health	9
3	Jobs and education	12
4	Other countries, other customs	16
5	The natural environment	18
6	News, trade and public services	21
7	Society, state, government	23
	Photocopiable Material	28
	Mock Exam Tasks	40
	Mock Exam Tasks – Answer Key	52
	Script for Listening Comprehension	54
	Answer Sheet	Inside Back Cover

Useful titles:

The European Language Certificates Certificate in English - Learning Objectives and Test Format (WBT 1998)

The European Language Certificates Certificate in English - Mock Examination 1 (WBT 1998)

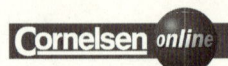 www.cornelsen-teachweb.de

INTRODUCTION

OVERALL LEARNING OBJECTIVES

Lift Off is a series of coursebooks leading learners to the *European Language Certificate/ Volkshochschul-Zertifikat* developed by the *Weiterbildungs-Testsysteme GmbH* (WBT), Frankfurt am Main, Germany.
At the end of *Lift Off 3* learners reach the level of Stage One *Grundbaustein* (See *The European Language Certificates Certificate in English – Learning Objectives and Test Format* (WBT 1998) p. 231 ff.). After completion of *Lift Off 4*, learners have acquired approx. 4000 words, they have learned the most important grammar structures and have met the most important idioms or idiomatic expressions used in the English language. On completion of *Lift Off 4*, having practised all the four skills, taught on the principles of learner centred teaching, learners could, in fact, sit the Stage Two examination (See *Learning Objectives* ... p. 236 ff.).

WHO IS LIFT OFF TO CERTIFICATE AIMED AT?

1. **Examination candidates**
   Working in co-operation with WBT, *Lift Off to Certificate* follows the format of the *European Languages Certificate*. As in the examination, the coursebook treats each of the four skills separately, using authentic or semi-authentic material similar to the material examinees will be faced with. In effect, *Lift Off to Certificate* offers specific practise for the Stage Two exam, culminating in a mock written examination. Working with *Lift Off to Certificate*, learners also become familiar with the format of the oral examination.

2. **Learners who wish to repeat and consolidate the four skills**
   These participants will have chosen to work with *Lift Off to Certificate* because they (or you as their long-time teacher) feel the need to practise the four skills separately, consolidating them before moving on to conversation.

Lift Off to Certificate may be used for both types of classes. While potential examinees will be working towards the deadline of the examination date, learners who are under less pressure can go through the material at a more leisurely pace. It is up to you as the teacher to ascertain what your students want and use the material accordingly.

THE STRUCTURE OF THE COURSEBOOK

Lift Off to Certificate comprises seven units, divided into two 90-minute sections. It also contains **files**, **photocopiable material**, an **answer key**, a **tapescript** and a **vocabulary list.**

Units 1 & 2 introduce learners to all of the elements that they will meet in the exam. These two units also include relevant information relating to the examination.
From **Unit 3** onwards, each unit is made up of a mixture of **conversation**, **listening**, **writing** and **reading** exercises. Each of the two 90-minute sections in **Units 3–7** begins with a **warm-up** which introduces and practises relevant vocabulary. The section then continues with one of the elements from the **oral examination**. We suggest that from **Unit 3** onwards you practise each of the oral exam activities as **mock oral examinations**. (See p. 12–13 of this teacher's book.) Command of discourse and co-operation strategies needed in face-to-face communication carries a lot of weight in the oral examination (See *Learning Objectives* ... p.74 ff.). These strategies are presented in the first listening exercise of each unit and learners are encouraged to learn and practise them throughout. Exercises which strictly follow the format of the examination are marked with their appropriate **examination logo**. None of the exercises is specifically designated as homework. It is suggested, however, that, from **Unit 3** on, letter writing and **Forward focus** can be done at home to be checked and discussed at the next lesson. There is one **CD** to be used both in class and at home.

The **Teacher's Book** includes **optional activities**, **time fillers** and suggestions for **discussion and debate**. You will find **photocopiable material** in this teacher's book. Helpful notes and background information have been included where necessary while, under the heading, **Teacher's needs**, we have included extra material or media, which should be organized before the start of the lesson.

Teaching a certificate course should not mean that the lessons are dry. While keeping to the set topics and tasks required for the Stage Two examination, we have used as many varied ways of introducing and handling the exercises as possible. Throughout the Teacher's Book you will occasionally come across the instruction, **Start this exercise with books closed**. Working without the coursebook encourages real communication and helps in effective listening. However, after doing an exercise with the coursebook closed, ensure that learners realize they have covered the material by asking them to look at the page(s) at home and compare them with their notes.

Similarly, we occasionally suggest that instead of having learners read questions for discussion from their books, the teacher should **dictate** the material. Here we are not only giving the learners the opportunity to train their listening but also to practise their writing. From a purely practical point of view, where the instruction is to walk around and ask other participants questions, it is easier to move round the classroom referring to a small piece of paper or a card rather than reading from the coursebook.

Speaking is not only an integral part of the examination, it is also the most useful form of communication in everyday life. **Role plays**, **partner** and **group work** promote the easy-going atmosphere required for speaking which learners will take with them beyond *Lift Off to Certificate* into the real world.

> **Note:** The listening section of the mock exam has not been recorded. You can find the transcript, which you can read out loud to the class, in the back of this teacher's book.

1 Hello, nice to meet you

1 It is unlikely that all the class has the coursebook but, even if everyone does have a copy of *Lift Off to Certificate* with them, you may wish to start the lesson without referring to the book.

Explain that the oral examination begins with **Social Contacts** in which candidates are invited to ask each other questions in order to find out as much as possible about each other (See *Learning Objectives* ... p. 250.). Ask the class: **What do you want to find out about someone the very first time you meet them?** Elicit two or three answers. Put the class into pairs and tell them they are going to interview each other then introduce their partner to the class. Suggest that they make a few notes about the other person. While learners are talking, walk around, listen and assess abilities.

When the interviews have come to an end, ask one member of the class to introduce his/her partner. Choose someone whose English is relatively good as a model. When the introduction is over, pick up on something that has been said and ask the partner a direct question relating to that topic. Encourage class members to ask something, too. Continue until everyone has been introduced and has had the opportunity to say something to the whole class.
Depending on whether the class knows you or not, you may wish to end this section by having the pairs think up two or three questions they would like to ask you.
When the questions come to an end, refer the class to the exercise they have just done in the book.

2 Lead-in
Indicate the pictures and speculate about the people, eg, job, lifestyle, hobbies, etc.

a Read out the first sentence of the instructions and suggest that, since we know what the people are going to be talking about, we might also be able to guess some of the words they might use. Make a list of possible words on the board. Leave the list up during the listening exercise.
Give the class time to read the names and statements. Tell learners to listen carefully, concentrate on the pictures and decide who is talking. The class should not write anything while listening. Play the exercise all the way through. In a strong class learners can match the names and statements immediately. If you have a weaker class, play each segment again and elicit the answers.

Now relate back to the list of words on the board. How many of them matched what was said?

b The WBT puts great emphasis on discourse markers (See *Learning Objectives* ... p. 201 ff.). In this exercise we are making our learners aware of markers for modifying or commenting on what is being said. Point out the examples: **now / now then; well / well then; as a matter of fact** and explain that, although these words look as if they do not really mean anything, they are quite useful for organizing, commenting or framing what we are saying or writing. Try to elicit more discourse markers and write them on the board, eg **so / so to speak; for example; for instance**. If necessary, give a few examples in German, eg *offen gesagt*; *zum Beispiel*; *freilich*.
Tell the class they are going to hear the **CD** again, this time listening out for the discourse markers which begin each statement. Stop the **CD** after each statement and elicit the answer from the class. Write the discourse marker on the board, then ask what function it has.

Key 1 You know ... – the speaker is going to make a suggestion and expects the listener to agree.
2 Actually ... – you may not believe what is going to come next, but it is true.
3 You see ... – begins an explanation.
4 Well ... – the speaker is aware that he is not giving the expected answer.
5 As far as I'm concerned ... – the speaker is offering her point of view.

c **Teacher's needs:** One copy per course participant of **Useful phrases** (p. 28 of this teacher's book).

Tell the class which of the people you have just heard you would like to / not like to share a flat with. Explain why, using an appropriate discourse marker. Then ask one of the class members who he/she would like to / not like to share a flat with. When that person has finished talking, have him/her ask another member of the class.
Distribute copies of **Useful phrases** and say that these phrases (or strategies) or discourse markers are important. Give the class time to look at them, discuss any questions which may come up, then tell the class to read and learn these phrases systematically at home. Check progress from time to time in the classroom.

3 Lead-in

Begin with closed books. Depending on the type of learners you have, ask: **Does anyone here have a flat mate? / Have you ever shared a flat. / Could you imagine sharing a flat with someone?** (We only want a yes/no answer here.) Then continue with: **You're thinking of sharing a flat with someone in this class.** Either get the class to open their books or, if you prefer the class to continue without reading from the book, dictate the six points. Put the class into pairs and get them talking. Stress that they should not interrogate each other – they are simply going to have a conversation and report their ideas to the rest of the class. While they are talking, walk around and listen. Do not correct mistakes but make a note of any particularly bad blunders (eg mixing up *since* and *for*). Before getting pairs to report back to the whole class, mention the mistakes you heard (without saying who made them) and have the whole class correct them.

When the activity has come to an end, tell the class that they have just practised another part of the oral examination (See *Learning Objectives* ... p. 250 ff.).

4 Lead-in

(See *Learning Objectives* ... p. 247 ff.)
Teacher's needs: slips of paper
Ask if anyone in the class has ever had a pen-friend. Divide the class into groups of three and give each person in the group a slip of paper bearing one of the names, Hazel, Frank or Marie. Each member of the group reads his/her advertisement, then tells the other two group members about his/her person. Check that everyone knows the names and hobbies of the three advertisers.

a Tell learners they are going to write to one of these people. They can choose any of the three, it need not necessarily be the person they read about. Stress that they should not tell anyone else who they are going to write to. Before they start to write, direct learners to **Greeting and closing formulas** on p. 7.
Now read out the four points that have to be included. Tell learners not to start the letter immediately, but make some notes. Give them three or four minutes to do this. Lastly, indicate the **general plan for letters** at the bottom of p. 6 and tell them to write their letter. Walk around and check for mistakes. Point out any problems and discuss, encouraging learners to correct their mistakes themselves.

b Remind learners that you are now going to guess the name of the addressee, so they should leave out the name at the beginning.

5 **Teacher's needs:** If **OHP** available, one blank transparency. If you do not have access to an **OHP**, use the board as instructed.

Ask the learners to read all three advertisements silently. When they have finished, check for vocabulary problems.
Decide as a class who you are going to write to and make notes at the top of the transparency. If no **OHP** available, use one half of the board, leaving notes up to refer to later. Tell learners that they should not write anything. Assure them that everyone will get their own copy of the letter.
Choose an appropriate greeting and begin the letter either on the transparency or on the other half of the board.
Work through the notes and write the letter together. End with an appropriate closing formula. Either photocopy the transparency for distribution in the next lesson or dictate the letter from the board.

6 **Lead-in**

Ask the class how they decide which articles they are going to read in a newspaper or magazine. Then ask learners to think about how they read an article when they are in a hurry. Many of them may know the word "skimming" already. If not, they will be able to describe what they do. Write "skimming" on the board. Now direct learners to the **TIP**. Insist that they follow the instructions for skimming, put them into pairs and get them started on the exercise. Check that all have the correct answers then ask one or two pairs to explain why they chose as they did.

Note: The commercial TV programme "Friends" follows the ups and downs of six thirty-something single people (three men, three women). The series started in 1995.

7 **Lead-in**

Teacher's needs: OHP copy of the text if **OHP** available (p. 29 of this teacher's book). If you do not have access to an **OHP**, then photocopies of the text (one per participant).

Start this section with books closed. Tell learners they are now going to read a text and pick out details. Explain how to go about reading for detail **(TIP)**. Reassure learners that, although this kind of reading takes longer than "skimming", there will be more than enough time in the examination to do this task properly and carefully.

If an **OHP** is available, tell the class that they are going to have one minute to read the text. Switch on the **OHP** for one minute then switch it off. If no **OHP** is available, distribute the photocopies, allow learners one minute to read the text then tell them to turn the photocopy over.
Now elicit words and phrases that people have seen in the text. Write them on one half of the board. When you have finished, the learners should open their books, cover the text and read through the multiple choice questions. Now decide together who or what the class has to find out about. Make a list on the other half of the board. There should be some similarity between both lists of words and phrases.
The class should now uncover the text in their books and complete the exercise. Check the answers then move on to **exercise 8**.

9 **Note**: This part of the exam contains 12 advertisements on up to three topics. We have reduced the number of items here, concentrating more on instructing learners how to do selective reading. Direct learners to the **TIP**, pointing out that they do this type of reading every time they look for a name in the telephone book.

Key Read the situations and mark key words:
1 cotton-covered settee; reduced; sales.
2 Low-priced; traditional; machine-washable covers.
3 Leather chair; delivered to Germany. Now read the titles and look at the pictures. Read the texts, marking key words. Complete the task and discuss the answers.

2 Hobbies and health

1 Warm-up

The class should begin with closed books while the teacher explains the tasks (**1a** and **1b**). Check that learners know what they have to do, then put them in pairs and tell them to open their books. Close books after 30 seconds and do both tasks. When everyone has finished, check and find out which pair has the most words. Then ask the class what their hobbies are. List the hobbies on the board and leave them up for the **lead-in** to **exercise 4**.

Alternative exercise: Hobby words brainstorming
Make groups of four and choose one member of the group as writer.

Proceed as follows:
a Each group draws three columns on a sheet of A4 paper. In the first column, make a list of all the hobbies that you know. Do not use more than three of the hobbies shown in the pictures. Stop writing after one minute.
b Pass the list to the group on your left. In the second column, beside the hobbies on your new list, write down what the people who do that hobby are called. Stop writing after one minute.
c Now pass this paper to the group on your left. This time, write down the names of the places where people do the hobby or the equipment they need. Use the third column. Stop after one minute.

Pass the paper back to its original group. Which group has the most words? Read them out.

2 Lead-in

Tell the class they are going to practise another part of the oral examination (See *Learning Objectives* ... p. 250 ff.). Stress that there is no right or wrong answer here, everyone should express his/her subjective opinion.

Put learners into pairs and designate each person **A** or **B**. Tell them that they have to choose a hobby for the person who made the statement they are going to read then direct them to their appropriate files at the back of the coursebook. While pairs are talking, go around and listen. Do not correct any mistakes but make a note of any particularly bad problems. Discuss these problems with the class as a whole before the reporting back stage. If appropriate, add more words to the list of activities on the board and leave the list up for **lead-in** to **exercise 4**.

3

a Play all the way through without stopping. Check the answers.

Key collecting teddy bears; in-line skating; photography, including developing and printing; living like Celts in the Middle Ages; playing music.

Note: Learners may express disbelief in the hobby which the fourth speaker talks about. The information comes from an article in *Positive News from around the World*, No. 15 Winter/Spring 1998. Two similar hobbies which are quite common in some parts of the UK and USA are living like North American Indians and "playing out" battles from long ago. Encourage discussion.

b Play the **CD** again, stopping after each phrase to allow class to tick. Check the answers.

c Provide a model by telling the class what you are going to do at the weekend.

4 Lead-in

Direct learners to the **Effective Listening TIP** at the top of p. 12 of the coursebook. Give them time to read through. Write the word **Anticipation** at the top of the board and ask the class if they can define what is meant by trying to anticipate what they are going to hear. The idea here is to get learners to find out for themselves what sort of things they can do before a listening exercise to make it easier.
If the group is weak, make a list of suggestions on the board under the following headings:

What do I want to find out by listening? Is it specific or general information? Do I have to listen for times, numbers, dates?
Who is talking? Are they men or women? How many people will be talking?
Where are they talking? Are the people in a formal or an informal situation? Language changes according to the degree of formality of the situation.

In a strong class have learners discuss in groups for some minutes then report back to the whole class. If you want, you can write the suggestions on the board.

Finally, for both strong and weak classes, refer to the last sentence in the box, "You can understand a listening exercise without knowing every word". Remind the class of the concept of "listening for gist" then move on to **4a**.

a Give learners time to read the instructions then play the **CD**. Check the answers.

b Ask for a show of hands on the various entertainment likes and put class into pairs accordingly. Give them some minutes to talk before reporting back to the class as a whole.

Optional activity: Discussion and debate

Teacher's needs: Role play cards on p. 30 of this teacher's book.

Divide the class into three groups, **A**, **B** and **C** and distribute the role play cards.
Check that learners know what they are supposed to do and allow the groups some minutes for preparation.
When everyone is ready, ask the speakers of the three groups to present their cases. Suggest that each group makes notes while their speaker is talking.
Have the groups evaluate their speaker then get feedback from the whole class. Who put forward the best case?

5 Lead-in

Indicate the picture and ask if anyone in the class belongs to an amateur dramatics group. If yes, allow the person a short amount of time to explain what plays his/her group performs. If no, ask as appropriate: is there an amateur dramatics group in the area? What sort of plays do these groups perform?
Note: *Bauerntheater* is rural folk theatre.
Draw learners' attention to the opening of the exercise, giving them time to read it before having them close their books.

a Write the word **Anticipation** on the board. Put class into pairs and get them to make a list of words/phrases they might expect to hear in the interview. After a few minutes have pairs report their lists of words. If you wish, you can write the words on the board.

b Let the class open their books and give learners time to read the sentences. Make sure that everything is clear then play the **CD**. Check the answers and, if necessary, replay the **CD** stopping at any problem points.

05 **6** **Lead-in**

Initiate a brainstorming session on what sort of things might come under the heading, **selective listening**, eg weather/traffic report; railway station announcement; radio announcement.
Give class time to read through the questions. Say that you will play each text twice, as in the examination, and tell the class to mark the answer after the second hearing. Play the **CD**. Check the answers, replaying the **CD** if necessary.

7 **Homework / Class exercise**

9 **Lead-in**

Draw the learners' attention to the first part of the **Learning Vocabulary TIP**, reminding them that it makes sense to collect topic-specific vocabulary then proceed to **exercise 9**. When you have finished, do **exercise 8** (See *Learning Objectives* ... p. 241 ff.). Put class into pairs and get them to do the exercise. Check the answers.

10 When learners have finished, check the answers, then draw their attention to second part of **Learning Vocabulary TIP**. Go through the letter piece by piece eliciting phrases which might be learned as a whole. Write the phrases on the board in such a way that you can add alternative words underneath. Suggest that certain words can be changed and add these words, eg *Despite specialist treatment/care/help; According to the terms of my contract / the guarantee*, etc.

11 **Homework / Class exercise**

12 **Homework**

Collect feedback at the start of the next lesson.

3 Jobs and education

1 Warm-up

Make sure that everyone understands what they have to do then put the class into groups of three. Go around and listen. When you hear that all of the group members have spoken about their "dream" job, encourage them to talk about what they really do. When the exercise is over and everyone has had a chance to report back, remind the class that questions about candidates' jobs are likely to come up in the oral examination.

2 Lead-in

Ask if anyone in the class has experience of job sharing. If yes, get the person/people to talk about the pros and cons. If no, try to elicit the pros and cons from the class as a whole.
If any members of the class have the same job, they might want to work together.

Suggestion: Practising for the oral examination

On completion of the **topic-based activity** in Unit 2, exercise 2, the class has met and practised all three elements of the oral examination (**social contacts**, Unit 1, exercise 1; **consensus-finding task**, Unit 1, exercise 3). You may wish to treat all further oral examination activities in the coursebook as mock oral exams. If so, proceed as follows:

Remind the class that they have met and practised all three elements of the oral examination (see above) and suggest that you could now continue with the oral examination elements as mock oral examination role plays.
Put learners into groups of four and allocate the role play cards which you will find on p. 31 of this teacher's book. Reassure the "examiners" that they will also have their chance to be "candidates" at a later date. In the case of an odd number of learners, remind the class that they may be examined as a threesome and hand out the **Candidate C** card. Give the learners time to read and understand their cards, sorting out any problems as necessary before starting. Remind the class that each of the parts of the oral examination takes approximately five minutes. When the time is up, stop the "examination". Ask **Examiner B** to show the notes he/she has made to the other members of his/her group. Give the learners time to discuss these problems together. Try to encourage constructive criticism. When each group has finished, ask if any of the candidates would like to report back to the whole class. Other class members may be able to give helpful advice and/or reassurance.

Setting up the mock oral examination role play

1   Once **Examiner A** has been chosen, show him/her the appropriate pages and file in the coursebook. If there is to be a third candidate, give **Examiner A** the relevant statement to be handed over to **Candidate C** at the appropriate time. Remind **Examiner A** that each stage of the oral examination should take five minutes; in the case of three candidates, seven minutes.

2   Make sure that **Examiner B** is ready to take notes during the course of the examination.

> **You are now ready to guide the class through the three stages of the examination as follows:**
>
> 1 **Part 1 – Social contacts: Examiner A** asks the candidates to find out as much as possible about each other (*see Breaking the ice – Social contacts* on p. 5 of the coursebook). After about three minutes (four minutes if you are examining three candidates) introduce one of the following topics as appropriate: hobbies; pets; interest in sport/fitness/entertainment.
>
> 2 **Part 2 – Topic-based conversation**. Use the oral examination tasks, *Education* (Unit 3, exercise 7), *Eating out* (Unit 4, exercise 2b) or *What's in the paper* (Unit 6, exercise 2). If you have three candidates, **Examiner A** should give **Candidate C** the appropriate statement which you will find on p. 32 of this teacher's book.
>
> 3 **Part 3 – Consensus-finding task**. Use *Job sharing* (Unit 3, exercise 2), *Planning a nature reserve* (Unit 5, exercise 2) or *Public people, private lives* (Unit 7, exercise 3).

3 Lead-in

Look at the photos and decide which jobs the people have. Ask which qualities might be necessary for each job.
Note: There are no lighthouse keepers any more as the job is now done by computers. For this reason, our lighthouse keeper speaks in the past.

06 a Check that learners know what they are listening for, then get them to close their books. Play the **CD** once then check.

Key doctor, newsreader
The doctor says that the main quality she needs is patience.
The newsreader says he started his career in Wales.

07 b Lead-in
This exercise looks closely at homographs. Before starting, ask the class if they noticed anything strange/funny about a couple of the words that that the speakers used in **3a**. Play the **CD** again, stopping after the doctor says **patience**. Write **patience** on the board then continue with the doctor's statement to the end. Wait for a second or two to see if someone picks up on the word **patients**. If not, write it on the board. Play the doctor's statement again completely. Then repeat **patience/patients** indicating the two different spellings as you say the words.
Now play the newsreader's statement, stopping after the word **Wales**. Once again, write the word on the board. Go on to the first mention of the word **whales** and stop the **CD**. The newsreader uses the words again, this time in the order **whales/Wales**. Indicate both spellings on the board as he says the words.
Play the newsreader's statement again. Ask if anyone can guess how his last sentence continues, " ... when I announced the **weather**, I pronounced **weather** ..." (He probably pronounced it whether [hwedh'ər].)

Continue as follows:
Point out the word **homonyms**. Some learners may know the word already. If not, explain that homonyms can be subdivided into a) **homographs** and b) **homophones**. What they have just heard were homophones, ie words which sound the same (or approximately the same) but are spelt differently. Write the words **homographs** and **homophones** on the board and underline **graphs** and **phones**. Write **patience/patients** and **Wales/whales** under **homophones**. Now explain that homographs are words which are written in the same way but are pronounced differently and have a different meaning.

Elicit examples and list them under the heading homographs, eg wound [waʊnd] [wuːnd]. Now continue with **3b** as instructed in the coursebook.

Optional exercises: See photocopiable material on pp. 33–35 of this teacher's book.

4 Give the class time to read through the instructions and the situations. Check that everyone understands the vocabulary and what they have to do before they start the exercise. Check the answers.

5 Homework / Class exercise

6 Warm-up

Do this with books closed. Try to elicit from learners what sort of things they might remember about their school days. Then dictate the questions. Get learners to walk around and talk to other people in the class. Remind them that they are talking to each other, not conducting a cross-examination. Try to make sure that learners talk to as many people as possible. When they have had enough time, get the class to report back. When you have finished, refer to the exercise in the coursebook.

7 See **Suggestion: Practising for the oral examination** on p. 12–13 of this teacher's book.

08 **8** Before starting the listening, do some anticipation preparation as suggested. Play the **CD**, then check.

As already mentioned, questions about candidates' jobs may come up in the oral examination. For this reason it makes sense to encourage learners to talk confidently about different aspects of their work/training, etc. Finish off this listening exercise by asking if anyone in the class has ever done re-training. If yes, was it useful? Was it interesting? If no, ask if anyone would consider doing re-training in order to get a different job. If yes, ask appropriate questions. If no, ask class to think about how they might answer these two questions if they were to come up in the oral examination. Ask them to make notes at home and report back in the next lesson.

9 Ask for a show of hands on the question, **Did John Maclean get the job?** Let the class read through the letter quickly to check, then have them complete the task. Check the answers.

10 Lead-in

Keeping the coursebooks closed, ask which members of the class have seen the film *The Full Monty*. Ask those who have seen the film to tell the story in a few words. Depending on how many have not seen the film, you may decide to do this as partner work, with learners in small groups or with the whole class. When everyone has finished, get the class to open their books and do the reading exercise.

11 Homework

Suggestion: Confident learners may wish to write the report. Insist on a maximum length of three hundred words. Correct any mistakes together with the learner during the following lesson (eg while other learners are doing **exercise 4**, telling the report writer to do that exercise at home). At the end of the lesson give the learner the opportunity to read out his/her report to the rest of the class. Encourage constructive criticism.

4 Other countries, other customs

1 **Lead-in**

Teacher's needs: Large sized cards in three different colours, eg yellow, pink, blue. You will need enough of each colour so that every learner has all three cards, **A**, **B**, **C**. Before you distribute the cards, mark a letter **A** on the yellow cards, a **B** on the pink cards and a **C** on the blue cards.

a   Start the lesson with books closed. Tell the class they are going to do short dictations on three different coloured cards. First, hand out the yellow cards and dictate the questions for Group **A**. Tell the class to lay their yellow cards aside for the moment and hand out the pink cards. Dictate the questions for Group **B**. Now lay the pink cards aside and hand out the blue cards. Dictate the questions for Group **C**. Everyone in the class now has three sets of question cards. Divide the class into three groups, **A**, **B** & **C** and proceed as instructed in the coursebook. Make sure that everyone understands that they are only to work with their group's question card. Ask learners to keep their sets of cards and use them for revision.

2   See **Suggestion: Practising for the oral examination** on p. 12–13 of this teacher's book.

09 **3** **Lead-in**

Look at the pictures and read out the names of the ingredients and utensils so that learners can get used to the sounds of the Japanese words. Continue with questions: **Has anyone in the class eaten sushi? Has anyone ever made it themselves?** And so on.

a   Now play the **CD**, allowing learners time to do the matching exercise. Check and proceed to exercise **3b**. Play the **CD** again, stopping after each of the organizing words. Make a list on the board and leave it up.

b   Give learners a few minutes to make some preparatory notes. While they are talking, walk around and listen for mistakes/problems. Interfere only if you hear that someone is not using text organizing words. When they have finished, ask learners to repeat each others' recipes.

4   Go through the principle of this exercise with the class, reminding them that they will have more than enough time in the examination to do it slowly and carefully. After checking the answers, direct learners' attention to **exercise 6** on p. 25.

5   Proceed with the questionnaire as instructed. When pairs have finished, have them report about each other to the class.

7 **Warm-up**

Follow instructions for the game as given in the coursebook.

8 **Lead-in**

Write **When in Rome, do as the Romans do** on the board and ask the class what the equivalent of this proverb is in German *(andere Länder, andere Sitten)*. Ask if anyone has stories to tell about habits they found strange/pleasant/frightening in another country. Have the class do the exercise then check the answers. If you want, you could now proceed to **exercise 10** on p. 27.

9 **Lead-in**

Hand out the questionnaire on p. 36 of this teacher's book and have learners ask each other the questions. Get feedback then put the class into pairs according to who has the highest number of **yes** answers; who has the next highest, etc. Proceed with the consensus-finding task (See **Suggestion: Practising for the oral examination** on p. 12–13 of this teacher's book.).

10 **Lead-in**

Make the A-OK sign and ask what it means in learners' country/countries. Ask for other gestures and their meanings. If you are from a different culture, show the class any gestures which are different. Encourage the class to talk about how these differences might cause problems before starting the exercise.

11 **Lead-in**

Write the words **ecological tourism** and **environmental tourism** on the board. Has anyone in the class any personal experience of these new forms of tourism? What is the general opinion?
Is ecological/environmental tourism viable?
Now have the class do the exercise then check the answers and get feedback.

5 The natural environment

Suggestion: At the end of this unit / start of **Unit 6** we ask learners to have a careful look at some English-language newspapers. For your convenience, you may wish to ask the class to provide the papers.

1 Warm-up

Teacher's needs: B5 sized pieces of paper with the names of animals written in large block capitals. Pins or sticky tape.

Note: Animal names given in the *Learning Objectives* ... vocabulary list are *cat, mouse, horse, lamb, turkey, fish, bird*. *Dog, cow, chicken, sheep* and *insect* are also given in the list but would not be appropriate for this game.

Suggestion: Teachers with little time for preparation may wish to ask the class to prepare the papers and stick them on each other's backs.
Before the learners start to walk about, get them to suggest the kind of questions they might want to ask, eg **Am I a pet? Do I live in the desert?** Stress that they are not allowed to ask directly, **What animal am I?**

2 Lead-in

If there is a nature reserve in your area, you may wish to start this part of the lesson by talking about ways of improving it. Alternatively, talk about nature reserves that people in the class have visited. If no one has ever been to a nature reserve, refer back to the article about **Kosi Bay** on p. 28 of the coursebook. Now put class into pairs and proceed.

3 Lead-in

(11)

Ask the class to translate the title of the exercise into German *(Wie ich schon sagte)* and ask them what function these superfluous sounding words have in a conversation. Elicit some more conversation-building expressions and write them on the board together with their function.

a Play the **CD** and check the answers.

b Play the **CD** again and check the answers.

Key 1 As I was saying ... – takes the conversation back to an earlier point.
2 If you ask me ... – I'm going to let you know my opinion (even though you may not want to hear it).
3 Come to think of it ... – something in the conversation makes the speaker realize that there may be a problem.
4 Talking of ... – starts a new topic which is linked to the present one.
5 That reminds me ... – something in the conversation jogs the speaker's memory.

4

a Read through the headlines with the class and get them to do the exercise. Check the answers.

b Ask the class for a show of hands to show who is interested in text 1, text 2, etc and have them make groups. Each group should choose one person as their writer.

c Ask groups to report to the whole class. Try to encourage a discussion.

5

a Have the class look at the picture and decide what is going on between the two birds. Now let them read the text and check that everyone has understood the vocabulary.

b Ask what sort of problems the birds might have, going through the list of sentences at **5c** and speculating if the "problems" mentioned might be true or false.

c As there are three people talking and the interview is rather long, get learners to close their books and play the **CD** once through without stopping. Elicit what the learners have heard in the first run-through, then, with books open, play the **CD** again, stopping at the relevant bits of information to allow the class to mark true or not true.
Allow time for discussion before moving on to **exercise 6**.

7

Check that the class understands the instructions and that everyone feels confident about doing the puzzle. Suggest that learners write the weather words directly onto the umbrella, ie under the symbols, and remind them that the boxes on the left are simply for taking note of the letters. If you think your learners might find the puzzle too demanding, there is an alternative exercise for you to photocopy on p. 37 of this teacher's book.

8

a Write the words **Climate in chaos** on the board and have the class decide together what the article is going to be about. Do some pre-teaching of the vocabulary by talking about interesting or chaotic weather in your area or any floods, droughts, etc mentioned in recent news bulletins.

b Continue with the discussion about extreme weather conditions, then put the class into pairs to do **exercise c**.

d Learners may have already given their views on this point at **8b**.

Optional activity

Write a reader's letter to the Australian newspaper agreeing or disagreeing with the article, *Climate in chaos*.

9

Follow instructions at **9a** and **9b** then practise the listening exercise as usual. Check the answers.

Optional activity

There is a jazz chant on p. 38 of this teacher's book.

10 Proceed as suggested in the coursebook.

11 **Lead-in**

You may wish to play the song first with books closed. Elicit from learners how much they have understood before having the class read the words and the short biography.

   a Do the exercise then check the answers.

   b Ask the class to listen to the song.

Optional activity: Use of English – creating moods

If your class has enjoyed the song and would like to do more intensive work with it, ask them how Ewan MacColl has created the mood of the song. Refer to **2c** in the multiple choice questions. Ask the class which of the words and phrases in the song have to do with **noise**. Make a list on the board. Now move on to words and phrases which suggest **movement** and finally to the ones which suggest **colour**.
Some of the phrases may turn up in more than one category. Depending on the abilities of the class, some learners may only be able to find one word for each category. In this case, ask them to try to picture what is going on in the song.

Elicit from the class the words for the five senses in English and write them on the board – **hearing**, **sight**, **smell**, **taste**, **touch**. Some of the words and phrases can go under these headings. Which of the other senses are conveyed in the song? Find more words and phrases and list them under their appropriate headings. Continue the lists until you have a good selection of words to do with the five senses.

Key

1 **Noise** – cats prowling; I heard a siren; making an axe; chop
   Movement – clouds drifting; cats prowling; springs a girl; train; wind; making an axe; chop
   Colour – clouds; moon; saw a train set the night on fire; shining steel; fire

2 **hearing** – see **noise** above
   sight – clouds drifting; saw a train
   smell – gasworks; canal; cats; smelled the spring; smoky; dead tree
   taste – kissed my girl
   touch – make a good sharp axe; chop; dead tree

12 **Homework**

Check that learners have newspapers or intend to buy some. Encourage people to buy different papers, including tabloids, so that the class can see as many as possible.

6 News, trade and public service

1 **Warm-up**

Teacher's needs: Selection of English-language newspapers.

a Point to the various newspapers in the photo at the beginning of the unit and ask the class which countries they are from. Encourage use of both noun and adjective, eg **Asia – Asian**.

Suggestion: If you have Internet access, you may wish to look at **Reading a British daily paper** at http://www.cornelsen-teachweb.de/liftoff.

Key Asia; Israel; USA; India; UK

Now continue as suggested in the coursebook, leaving the list of titles up for the **topic-based activity**, **exercise 2**.

b If no one has prepared a presentation, divide the class into as many groups as you have newspapers. Give each group one newspaper and tell them to go through it carefully making notes on **style**, **content**, **headline language**, etc. When they have done that, they should choose one article together and read it, making notes on what it is about. The groups should then present their newspaper to the rest of the class.

2 Put the class into pairs and proceed.

3 **Lead-in**

After the "hands-on" practice with the various newspapers, learners should now have a good idea of the differences between broadsheet and tabloid paper language. Ensure that the class knows the word **slang** and try to elicit some examples which they may have seen in their papers. Make sure that the class realizes that tabloids use a lot of slang. Now write the word **pun** on the board and ascertain if anyone can give an example of a pun in German. Some exceptional learners may be able to give an example in English. If no one knows what a pun is, write the following on the board: The asparagus in the restaurant was very expensive, but at least it included the tip. ("tip" means both *Spargelspitze* and *Trinkgeld*). Remind learners that *The Guardian* is famous for its puns.

a Tell the class to listen and note down any words they find helpful. Play the **CD** all the way through. Do not ask for the final answer yet but have learners show their words and explain their ideas to the person sitting beside them. When they have finished talking, play the **CD** through again, this time stopping after every dialogue in order to decide together if the paper is a broadsheet or a tabloid. Ask the learners to explain the reasons for their choice.

b Refer learners to the box of compensation strategies at the beginning of the exercise before you play the **CD** again. When you have finished, check the answers then go on with **3c**.

4 If you have a **mixed class**, let the learners look over the questionnaire, check for vocabulary or other problems, then get them to do the exercise all the way through. If your class is made up purely of **business people**, change the first question in the box to to: *Which of the following would you like to eliminate from your life? Why?* In this case, leave out the last two questions in the box, *Would you like to have any of the things mentioned above? Why / Why not?*

5 Depending on the length of time taken up by **exercise 4**, you may wish to set this exercise as homework to be checked at the next lesson.

6 Homework / Class exercise

7 Warm-up

Brainstorming: Talk about various shops, boutiques, factory outlets, etc in your area. Now get the learners to read the introduction to **Are you a shopaholic** before doing the "test" quickly, answering spontaneously. They should not take anything too seriously. Talk together as a class about the results. You may wish to use the results to organize the learners into pairs for **exercise 8**.

Optional activity: Words which take the suffix "-aholic".
If you find it suitable, you may wish to start off this exercise by looking at various words which take the suffix **-aholic**. Write the word **shopaholic** on the board, underlining the suffix. Ascertain that learners know what the word means then continue with other **-aholic** words and their meanings.

9 Still in their pairs, give the class time to go through the letter and the multiple choice vocabulary. Check that everyone understands, then have them do the exercise. Check the answers.

10 Play the **CD** through once. In a **strong class** the learners may be able to tick the appropriate boxes immediately. In a **weaker class**, play the **CD** through once more, stopping after each statement. Check then go on to **10b**.

11 Ask the class to look at the photograph and the sub-headline. Ascertain that everyone knows the word *Romany* then invite the class to pre-guess the information that might be in the text. Make notes on the board. Tell learners to read the text quickly then compare with the notes on the board before answering the multiple choice questions.

12 Homework

7 Society, state, government

1 Warm-up

Suggestion: In case class members cannot agree, check the current answers to the first two items before the lesson.

Key to the abbreviations: PM, Prime Minister; UN, United Nations; MP, Member of Parliament; NATO, North Atlantic Treaty Organization; EU, European Union; OPEC, Organization of Petroleum Exporting Countries; ANC, African National Congress.

2

a Check that learners know these women and when they lived. Then read the names of their "partners". Match the couples before doing the listening exercise.

Notes:
Marilyn Monroe (1926–1962), US film actress. She made clever comedies such as *Gentlemen Prefer Blondes* (1953), *How to Marry a Millionaire* (1953), *The Seven Year Itch* (1955), *Bus Stop* (1956), and *Some Like It Hot* (1959).
Born in Los Angeles to a single mother who was often confined in mental institutions, Marilyn Monroe had a wretched childhood. She married for the first time at the age of 16, her second husband was baseball star Joe DiMaggio, and her third was playwright Arthur Miller, who wrote *The Misfits* (1960) for her, a serious film that became her last. Marilyn Monroe committed suicide, taking an overdose of sleeping pills.

John F Kennedy: (1917–1963) 35th president of the USA (1961–1963), a Democrat; the first Roman Catholic and the youngest person to be elected president. In foreign policy he carried through the unsuccessful Bay of Pigs invasion of Cuba, and secured the withdrawal of Soviet missiles from the island in 1962. His programme for reforms at home, called the New Frontier, was posthumously executed by Lyndon Johnson. Kennedy was assassinated while on a visit to Dallas, Texas, on 22 Nov 1963. Lee Harvey Oswald (1939–1963), who was shot dead a few days later by Jack Ruby (1911–1967), was named as the assassin.
In 1953 Kennedy married socialite Jacqueline Lee Bouvier (1929–1995).

The imaginary telephone conversation refers to Kennedy's birthday party in May, 1962 in Madison Square Gardens. At the party Marilyn Monroe, wearing an almost see-through dress, sung "Happy Birthday, Mr President".

Anne Boleyn (1507–1536) Queen of Henry VIII and mother of Queen Elizabeth I of England. Anne was maid-in-waiting to Catherine of Aragon (Henry's first wife) and became her successor when Catherine's marriage was annulled. Anne Boleyn failed to produce a male heir for Henry and was beheaded on a charge of adultery.

Henry VIII (1491–1547) King of England. Came to the throne in 1509. He was a skilled musician and sportsman but is most often remembered for being married six times. He was the father of Edward VI, Mary I and Elizabeth I.

The imaginary telephone conversation refers to Henry's favoured way of disposing of his unwanted wives.

Wallis Simpson, Duchess of Windsor (1896–1986). Wallis Simpson was a US socialite, twice divorced. She married Edward VIII of Britain in 1937. Edward abdicated in order to marry her.

Duke of Windsor, Edward VIII (1894–1972). He was given the title Duke of Windsor by his brother, George VI, who succeeded him.

The imaginary telephone conversation refers to Mrs Simpson's love of fashion.

c If your learners have problems deciding who to choose, you will find a list of couples on p. 39 of this teacher's book. Either copy for the **OHP** or read the list out.

3 See **Suggestion: Practising for the oral examination** on p. 12–13 of this teacher's book.

4 Give the class time to read the five texts and the headings. The class may wish to talk about some or all of the topics reported in the texts.

5

a If the class appears uncomfortable with the subject, move on to **5b**.

b Give the class time to read the instructions and the sentences. Tell the class just to listen and play the **CD** all the way through without stopping. Make sure that everyone has understood the gist of the radio programme then play the **CD** again, stopping as necessary to allow learners to mark true or not true. Check the answers before moving on to **5c** if appropriate.

6 Homework / Class exercise

7 Warm-up

If you put the class into pairs for this exercise, no one will feeling that they, personally, are in a stupid or embarrassing situation. Distribute the situations and allow pairs to work on them for two or three minutes. Now ask each pair to explain their situation and tell the others their excuse. Do other class members have a better excuse?

8 Lead-in

Is there a lot of crime in your area? If yes, discuss and talk about any ideas to combat the problems. If no, talk about crime in general. Is it increasing in your country? You may wish to refer back to **exercise 4, text 2** in this unit.

9 See **Suggestion: Practising for the oral examination** on p. 12–13 of this teacher's book.

10 Proceed as instructed in the coursebook.

Play the **CD** all the way through without stopping. Learners should be able to mark true or not true at the first hearing. Check the answers. If there are any problems, play the **CD** again.

11 Allow learners time to read the text and the answers then do the exercise. Since religion is sometimes a tricky subject of discussion you may wish to move on immediately to talking about revision.

12 Go through the four suggestions for revision, asking learners to choose at least two that they would like to do. Put like-minded learners into groups and have them discuss together how they are going to go about their revision. Perhaps some learners would like to meet outside the classroom and work together?

APPENDIX

Photocopiable Material .... pages 28–39

Mock Exam Tasks for The European Language Certificates –
Certificate in English

Reading Comprehension .... pages 40–45

Language Elements .... pages 46–47

Listening .... pages 48–50

Letter Writing .... page 51

Answer Key .... pages 52–53

Script for Listening Comprehension .... pages 54–56

Answer Sheet .... Inside Back Cover

Useful phrases

Read and learn these words and phrases. Try to practise them at every opportunity.

Opening a conversation
Do you know ...?
Do you remember ...?
Have you heard about ... ?
Did I ever tell you about ... ?

Ending a conversation
Right ...
That's it, then.
There we are.
Well, it's been nice talking to you.
See you soon.
Have a nice day.

Expressing an opinion
I think (that) ...
I believe (that) ...
I feel that ...
Well, in my opinion ...
If you ask me, ...

Generalizing
On the whole ...
By and large ...
Generally speaking ...
It's said that ...
As a rule ...
I have heard (that) ...

Expressing exceptions
There are exceptions, of course.
On the other hand ...
Don't forget (that) ...
You have to take into account (that) ...

Making assumptions
I suppose (that) ...
It could be (that) ...
I have the feeling (that) ...
I imagine (that) ...

Expressing certainty
I'm sure.
I'm certain about that.
Definitely.

Expressing uncertainty
I'm not sure.
I'm not so certain about that.
I may be wrong, but ...

Agreeing
I think so, too.
I agree completely.
That's exactly what I think.
Of course.

Disagreeing
I'm sorry, I can't agree with you there.
I see what you're getting at, but ...

Encouraging someone to continue
Go on.
Don't let me interrupt you.
And then?
So, what happened next?

Interrupting politely
I'm sorry to interrupt you, but ...
Can I just butt in here?
Sorry. I'd just like to say ...

Top Towns

Want to find a rich friend, go to the theatre or simply shop till you drop? Follow this guide to the best places in Britain to get what you want.

A survey conducted in the UK in June 1999 discovered that Liverpool has the most theatres, Manchester the most concert halls and Birmingham the most cinemas. But for the highest concentration of the arts of all types head for London's Westminster or Strathclyde in Scotland.

If you're a shopaholic, you should move to Gateshead, home to the UK's biggest shopping centre. Or go to Taunton in Somerset or Sefton in Merseyside. After London's Oxford Street, these two English towns have the largest amount of retail space per head in Britain.

Anyone looking for rich friends and neighbours must move to the London borough of Kensington and Chelsea, which has an average annual income of £44,722 per head of household. Outside London, Britain's richest can be found in Surrey and Berkshire where many of the houses are owned by pop stars and other showbusiness people.

If singing's your thing, why not move to Wales? 67% of Welsh people sing in choirs and the Welsh capital, Cardiff, has 22 male voice choirs with more than 30 members.

On the other hand, if it's fresh air and sport you're interested in, then Scotland is the place to be. Go to St Andrews for the best golf course in Britain; the River Tay for fishing in Britain's cleanest river; or to the Scottish Borders where you can learn to ride at one of the 16 riding schools – the biggest concentration of riding schools in the UK. Scotland is also the best place in Britain to be ill. Hypochondriacs should move immediately to the Scottish Highlands, the Orkney Isles or the Shetlands, where patient to doctor ratios are lowest.

Unit 2, Exercise 4b, Optional activity: Discussion and debate role play cards

Group A

Discussion: You enjoy going to the cinema. Decide together why this is the best form of entertainment. Make some notes.

Debate: Choose a speaker from your group to present your case to the rest of the class. The speaker should not talk for more than five minutes.

Evaluation: While your speaker is talking, listen and judge how well he/she is presenting your arguments. Make some notes.

Feedback: In your groups tell your speaker what you thought about his/her presentation. Perhaps you can give him/her some helpful advice?

Conclusion: Decide with the whole class which speaker put forward the best case.

Group B

Discussion: You enjoy going to the theatre. Decide together why this is the best form of entertainment. Make some notes.

Debate: Choose a speaker from your group to present your case to the rest of the class. The speaker should not talk for more than five minutes.

Evaluation: While your speaker is talking, listen and judge how well he/she is presenting your arguments. Make some notes.

Feedback: In your groups tell your speaker what you thought about his/her presentation. Perhaps you can give him/her some helpful advice?

Conclusion: Decide with the whole class which speaker put forward the best case.

Group C

Discussion: You enjoy staying at home to watch TV. Decide together why this is the best form of entertainment. Make some notes.

Debate: Choose a speaker from your group to present your case to the rest of the class. The speaker should not talk for more than five minutes.

Evaluation: While your speaker is talking, listen and judge how well he/she is presenting your arguments. Make some notes.

Feedback: In your groups tell your speaker what you thought about his/her presentation. Perhaps you can give him/her some helpful advice?

Conclusion: Decide with the whole class which speaker put forward the best case.

Instructions and role play cards for Oral Mock Exam

Examiner A

You are the examiner who asks the candidates the questions. You should not talk too much. Do not correct any mistakes.

1. Introduce yourself and the other examiner.
2. Explain that you will be asking some questions and that the other examiner will be listening.
3. Tell the candidates to ask each other questions to find out as much as possible about each other. Allow them five minutes for this task. (If there is a third candidate, your teacher will give you extra instructions.)
4. Ask the candidates to look at the appropriate page in the coursebook and begin the task. After five minutes, ask them to stop.
5. Thank the candidates and say goodbye.

Examiner B

You are the examiner who takes note of any mistakes that the candidates may make. After you have said hello to the candidates, do not speak to them any more until it is time to say goodbye.
The candidates should not see what you are writing during the examination. After the examination show the candidates the mistakes that you have noted down and talk together as a group about these problems.

Candidate A

Do the tasks the examiner gives you. Remember to talk only to the other candidate(s) while you are doing the tasks.

Candidate B

Do the tasks the examiner gives you. Remember to talk only to the other candidate(s) while you are doing the tasks.

Candidate C

Do the tasks the examiner gives you. Remember to talk only to the other candidate(s) while you are doing the tasks.

Third candidate
Extra statements for Candidate C

Education (Unit 3, Exercise 7)

Candidate C

1. Read the following statement:
   "Too many people never pick up a book again when they've finished school or university. But why should you stop finding out about new things just because you're done with formal education? Learn a foreign language; how to repair your car. Discover new things on the Internet. You should never stop learning."
2. Look at the pictures on p. 20 and decide which person could have made this statement.
3. Prepare to tell your partners about this person's opinion and why you have chosen him/her.
4. Finally, tell your partners your own opinion.

Eating out (Unit 4, Exercise 2b)

Candidate C

1. Read the following statement:
   "Cooking's my hobby so I always like to test new restaurants. I'm always looking for ideas. If the chef's made something I've never cooked myself, I usually try it out at home a couple of days later."
2. Look at the list of local restaurants on the board and decide where you could send the person who made the above statement.
3. Prepare to tell your partners about this person's opinion and which restaurant you have chosen for him/her.
4. Finally, tell your partners your own opinion.

What's in the paper? (Unit 6, Exercise 2)

Candidate C

1. Read the following statement:
   "I'm very busy but I need to keep up with changes on the market, so the only thing I read in the paper is the stocks and shares. I catch up with the rest of the news on TV in the evening."
2. Look at p. 35 and decide which newspaper the person who made this statement reads.
3. Prepare to tell your partners about this person's opinion, which newspaper you have chosen for him/her and why.
4. Finally, tell your partners your own opinion.

Unit 3, Exercise 3

Homonym tongue twisters

Cut up and distribute. Who can say their tongue twister fastest?

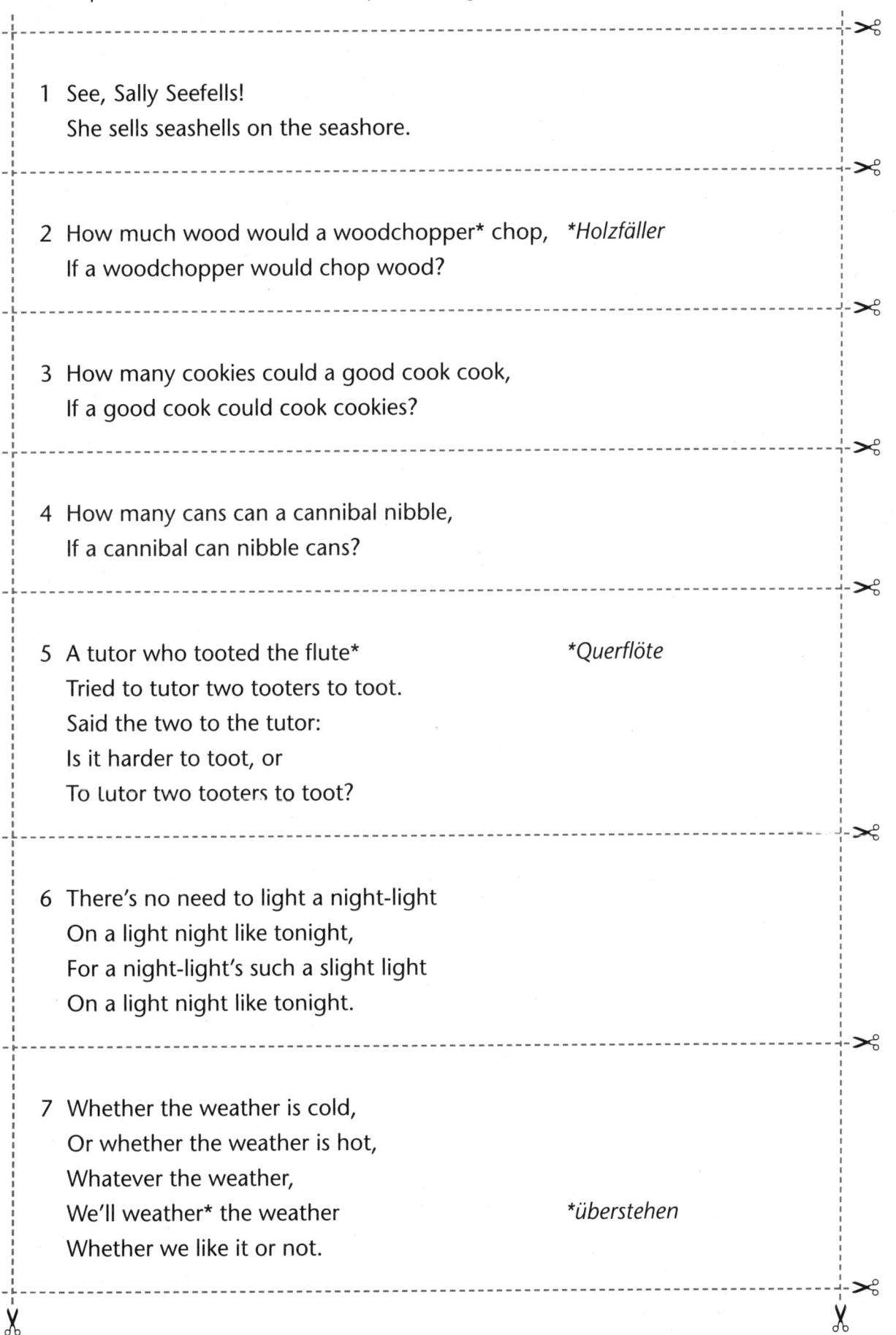

1 See, Sally Seefells!
  She sells seashells on the seashore.

2 How much wood would a woodchopper* chop,   *Holzfäller
  If a woodchopper would chop wood?

3 How many cookies could a good cook cook,
  If a good cook could cook cookies?

4 How many cans can a cannibal nibble,
  If a cannibal can nibble cans?

5 A tutor who tooted the flute*   *Querflöte
  Tried to tutor two tooters to toot.
  Said the two to the tutor:
  Is it harder to toot, or
  To tutor two tooters to toot?

6 There's no need to light a night-light
  On a light night like tonight,
  For a night-light's such a slight light
  On a light night like tonight.

7 Whether the weather is cold,
  Or whether the weather is hot,
  Whatever the weather,
  We'll weather* the weather   *überstehen
  Whether we like it or not.

Unit 3, Exercise 3

8 A woman to her son did utter*: *(altmodisch) sagen
   Go, my son, and shut the shutter.
   The shutter's shut, the son did mutter,
   I cannot shut it any shutter.

9 Of all the felt* I ever felt**, *Filz
   I never felt a piece of felt **tastete
   Which felt the same as that felt felt,
   When I first felt the felt of that felt hat.

10 Your Bob owes our Bob a bob*. *(slang) britisch Schilling
   If your Bob doesn't give our Bob
   The bob your Bob owes our Bob,
   Our Bob will give your Bob a bob** on the nose. **Schlag

11 All I want is a proper cup of coffee,
   A proper cup of coffee in a copper coffee pot.
   If I don't get a proper cup of coffee
   In a proper copper coffee pot,
   I probably will pop my top*. *ausflippen

12 Peter Piper picked a peck* of pickled pepper *Viertelscheffel
   Off a painted plate.
   If Peter Piper picked a peck of pickled pepper
   Off a painted plate,
   Where was the peck of pickled pepper
   Peter Piper picked?

Sentences with homophones

Put class into pairs and distribute the following

Partner A

Do not show these sentences to your partner. Read them out loud and ask your partner to write them down. Now check that he/she has spelt the homophones correctly.

They're reading in the garden. They took their books out there.
Do you think this is the right way to write it?
Our train leaves in one hour.

When you and your partner have written and checked both sets of sentences, think of some more homophones together. Use them to write sentences for another pair of learners.

Partner B

Do not show these sentences to your partner. Read them out loud and ask your partner to write them down. Now check that he/she has spelt the homophones correctly.

Wait till I check the weight of the parcel.
It's time to take the dog out. It's been wagging its tail for ages.
You're not allowed to read aloud in the library.

When you and your partner have written and checked both sets of sentences, think of some more homophones together. Use them to write sentences for another pair of learners.

Unit 4, Exercise 9

Find someone who ...

enjoys going on holiday by car.

likes coach holidays.

dislikes sunbathing.

hates sightseeing.

has been on a cycling holiday.

has never flown.

has travelled round the world.

has been to the USA.

has been to Australia.

has never had a holiday outside of their native country.

has lived for some time in a foreign country.

has had a holiday which lasted for more than four weeks.

Do you enjoy/like/dislike/hate ... ?

Have you ever ... ?

Unit 5, Exercise 7

A poem for April

Work with a partner and unscramble these weather words.

S H E R A L I S R W O P • R H U T D E N • I N R A • N I N G I R A • S L O U C D
S N E N W Y A T H R E U • B R A I N W O • D N I W • G I S W O N N • Y L C D O U

Look at this poem based on a 1920s song.
Decide with your partner which of the words fit. (Some of the words are used more than once. Others are not used at all.)

Though _ _ _ _ _ _ _ _ _ _ _ _ may come your way,

They bring the flowers that bloom in May.

So when it's _ _ _ _ _ _ _ , have no regrets,

Because it isn't _ _ _ _ _ _ _ _ _ _ _ , you know,

It's _ _ _ _ _ _ _ violets.

And when you see _ _ _ _ _ _ upon a hill,

You soon will see clouds of daffodil.

So keep on looking for a _ _ _ _ _ _ _ ,

You know it won't be long,

Whenever _ _ _ _ _ _ _ _ _ _ _ _ come along.

Now choose one of the following activities with your partner:

1 Think up some weather words or phrases. Scramble them and give them to another pair. Can they find out the words?
2 What is the "message" of the poem? Do you agree with it? Why (not)? Make up a weather rhyme or song with the opposite "message".

---✂

Key:

| April showers | thunder | rain | raining | clouds |
| sunny weather | rainbow | wind | snowing | cloudy |

Though April showers may come your way,
They bring the flowers that bloom in May.
So when it's raining, have no regrets,
Because it isn't raining rain, you know,
It's raining violets.
And when you see clouds upon a hill,
You soon will see clouds of daffodil.*
So keep on looking for a rainbow,
You know it won't be long,
Whenever April showers come along.

* poetic licence – daffodil does not take an /s/ in the plural here as it has to rhyme with "hill"

Unit 5, Exercise 9

A jazz chant

Group A	Group B
Winter weather Winter weather	Snow, sleet Icy cold
Spring weather Spring weather	Wind, hail Gusty showers
Summer weather Summer weather	Hot sun Thundery clouds
Autumn weather Autumn weather	Fog, haze Blustery breezes
Weather, weather Spring, summer	Winter weather Autumn weather

A & B together

Weather, weather, weather, weather.
We have to weather* every weather.

* überstehen

Unit 7, 2c Famous couples

- Romeo & Juliet
- Robin Hood & Maid Marian
- Mephistopheles & Faust
- Judy & Punch
- Prince Charles & Camilla Parker Bowles
- Dr Jekyll & Mr Hyde
- Captain Kirk & Mr Spock
- Snoopy & Charlie Brown
- Tristan & Isolde
- John Lennon & Paul McCartney
- Cleopatra & Antony
- Lancelot & Guinevere
- Dana Scully & Fox Mulder
- Winnie the Pooh & Christopher Robin
- David & Goliath
- Adam & Eve
- Steffi Graf & André Agassi
- Professor Higgins & Eliza Doolittle
- Don Quixote & Sancho Panza
- Margaret Thatcher & Ronald Reagan

1 Reading Comprehension – Part 1: Reading for Gist

Read the five texts, items 1–5. Then read the correct headlines A–J. Decide which headline A–J goes best with which text.
Mark your answers on the answer sheet (see Inside Back Cover).

1 A new-born baby was found yesterday abandoned on a doorstep. Police in Hull said the baby girl, who is thought to have been born yesterday, was taken to hospital but was well. The girl, who was wrapped in a pink shawl, was found in a box on an elderly woman's doorstep by a paper boy.

2 A 105-year-old retired Swiss school teacher received an order to attend elementary school when a computer cut a century off his age. Born in 1893, the man earlier this year joined 65 local five-year-olds for their first school day.

3 Women in Britain want their own version of the anti-impotence drug Viagra so they can spice up their sex lives, a survey reveals. Women say the main reason they want it is to improve their sex lives, and would even take their partner's pills.

4 Leeds Council is to spend £20,500 to knock two houses into one to make a six-bedroom "super-home" for a single mother and her ten children. The woman and children, aged from 15 months to 17 years, are now living in a four-bedroom house. She has been looking after them alone for eight years.

5 More than 1,000 passengers were stuck on a British ferry in Calais yesterday after striking ferry workers prevented them from disembarking. The passengers had to stay on board a P&O ferry for more than an hour, but finally were allowed to get off shortly after midday.

A **Bigger house for big family**

B **British women want anti-baby pills**

C Computer problem: 65 children miss first day at school

D **Ferry strike keeps tourists on land**

E Lost paper boy found on doorstep

F **Mother leaves 10 children alone at home**

G **One-day old child found safe and healthy**

H **Pensioner goes back to school**

I **Tourists had to wait on ship**

J **Women want similar pills to men**

1 Reading Comprehension – Part 2: Reading for Detail

Read the following two texts, then choose the answers to questions 6–10 and mark your answer – a, b, or c – on the answer sheet.

TEXT 1

Happy times are here for men as they keep hands off housework

66 per cent of British men are happier than they were five years ago, according to a survey out today.

But while men are beginning to give more support in doing housework, women are still the main workhorses in the home, reveals the report.

The survey also finds that marriage or moving in with a partner appears to be more stressful than divorce or ending a relationship. Two out of three men who have married in the last five years say their lives are stressful, compared with 53 per cent of those who have divorced or ended a relationship.

Young single men are among those most likely to find life stressful and are most in need of their friends. But despite this, three out of four of them are happier than they were five years ago.

Breaking out of normal routines is still the biggest cause of stress for young men – those who have recently left full-time education or who have moved out of their parents' home are most likely to feel stress.

Answer the following from the information given in the text.

6 British men
   a are doing as much work around the house as women.
   b are not doing as much work in the house as women.
   c think they do not have to help in the house at all.

7 According to the report
   a married men are less stressed than men living alone.
   b men living alone are unhappier than married men.
   c getting divorced is not as stressful as getting married.

8 Life is most stressful for young men
   a who are experiencing changes in their lives.
   b who have a busy social life.
   c who have lost their jobs.

1 Reading Comprehension – Part 2: Reading for Detail

TEXT 2

Read the following text.

Is this baby the youngest passport holder?

A BABY who was issued with a passport when he was just nine days old is believed to be the youngest Briton to hold one.

Blair Allan was less than a week old when his amazed parents, Suzanne and Gregor, were told that new regulations meant he would need a passport in his own name before he could return to his family home in Dubai, where his father is director of restaurants for Marriott Hotels.

His 31-year-old mother had flown back to Britain to give birth. 'I did it so Blair would get a British passport when he is older,' she said yesterday. 'I didn't expect he would need one this soon.' Blair's five-year passport contains a sleepy photograph of him. Now four weeks old, his appearance has already changed. Passport rules were changed in Britain two days before Blair was born. It is now compulsory for children under 16 to have their own passport if they are not already listed on their parents'.

Answer the following from the information given in the text.

9 The baby needed a passport
   a because his father works abroad.
   b because his parents are not British.
   c in order to leave Britain with his mother.

10 Blair will need a new passport
   a when he is five.
   b when he is sixteen.
   c when he needs a new photo.

1 Reading Comprehension – Part 3: Selective Reading

Read questions 11–20 and then look at the advertisements A–L on the following pages. In which advertisements can you find what you are looking for?

For each of the items 11–20, decide which advertisement goes with the situation described. Mark your answers on the answer sheet.

11 You want to work in another country and you need a brochure giving you a choice of offers.

12 You are interested in activity holidays and want to phone to get some information.

13 You want a brochure with recommendations on good hotels.

14 You live alone but want to meet other people during your holidays.

15 You and your partner want to stay in a hotel with a special price offer where you can swim in the hotel and where there are organized evening events.

16 You want to stay in a hotel that offers you a special price and from which you can see the sea.

17 For your theatre evening out you want to enjoy a meal in a nice restaurant.

18 You are looking for a restaurant which offers special fish and meat dishes.

19 You are looking for an old, high-class restaurant which is open for Sunday lunch.

20 You want to have a meal in a good restaurant in the middle of town where prices are not too high.

1 Reading Comprehension – Part 3: Selective Reading

Advertisements

A

EXPLORE worldwide

STOP PRESS! New brochure out now

Small groups exploratory holidays to fire your imagination from 1999 to the new millenium

- Cultural Tours
- Wildlife Safaris
- Easy Hikes
- Wildness Trips
- River Journeys
- Mountain Treks
- Tribal Encounters
- Sail & Seatreks

call now for our 126 page colour brochure
01252 522 100

Over 200 original adventures to 96 countries from the UK's leading adventure holiday specialist. 8 days to 6 weeks. From £335 to £2000 plus. Explore Worldwide (IN). Aldershot, GU11 1LQ www.explore.co.uk Fully Bonded AITO/ATOL 2595

B

2 FOR THE PRICE OF 1

YES – HALF PRICE!
incl. DINNER and ALL YOU CAN EAT full English Breakfast
ALSO FANTASTIC 2 FOR 1 DRINKS OFFER
139 En-suite Bedrooms. Htd Indoor Pool, Dancing Nightly.
27th Nov – LIVE!
The Searchers in Cabaret
Free admission for residents.
Include Sunday for only £12ppDBB

RAINBOW INTERNATIONAL HOTEL
Belgrave Road, Torquay
4 Crown Commended
01803 21 4343
Quoting Daily Mail

C

ARE YOU SPORT ENOUGH TO EARN £25,000 A YEAR?

If you keep fit, look good and like a challenge, if you are 18 or over, own a car and have access to a phone, if you are prepared to work hard for a high income, this advertisement is for you.

We are an international insurance company requiring three extra representatives in this area. No experience necessary as full training is given. Leads provided

Please ring 01978 735671

D

Unbeatable value French cuisine

Pierre Victoire

Enjoy lunch or dinner in our city centre authentic bistro offering a relaxed atmosphere, fabulous food & fine wines

- Daily changing à la carte menu
- Inexpensive French cuisine
- Set price business lunch menu
- Endless new ideas from our chefs

Voted restaurant of the year 1996

VISA   MasterCard

E

Overtures Restaurant

A LA CARTE – SET MENU – WIDE RANGING WINE LIST

SET IN ATMOSPHERIC SURROUNDINGS OPPOSITE THE NEW VICTORIA THEATRE
SPECIAL THEATRE/DINNER PACKAGES AVAILABLE

MasterCard   VISA

F

The Collection
Quality Hotel in Premier Locations
A superb selection of 3, 4 and 5 star hotel
Scheduled day flights,
from Gatwick & Heathrow
Free guide book and discount card
Deals, children, singles, honeymooners
Flexible duration from 2-56 nights
Price pledge:
We will not be beaten!
Voted Best Specialist Short Haul
Tour Operator 1997 & 1998

CADOGAN HOLIDAYS
24hr BROCHURE HOTLINE
0808 172424

1 Reading Comprehension – Part 3: Selective Reading

Advertisements

G

A NEW CAREER ABROAD

Travel may broaden the mind – but working abroad broadens the bank balance and the experience too. Every two weeks, Overseas Job Express carries over 1,500 opportunities from IT and Executive to Sales and Seasonal, plus all the latest news. For just £19.95, Overseas Job Express will be delivered to your door for 3 months. Order now. Cheque/PO/Credit Card details to Overseas Job Express, ref. ST, Premier House, Shareham Airport BN43 5FF. Or call 01273 340110. Credit Card Hotline 01273 353522 (24hrs).

OVERSEAS JOB EXPRESS

H

SINGLE?

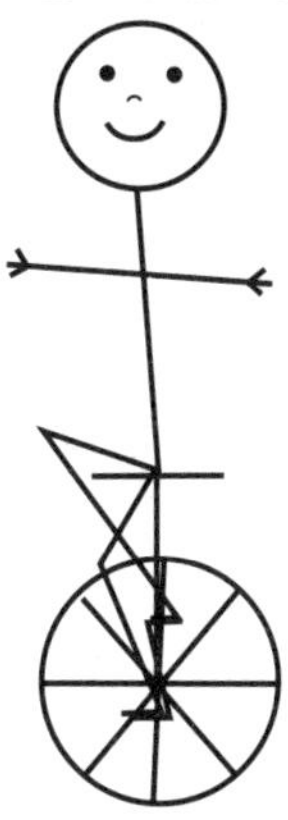

Why travel alone? Join a group with Solo's, the specialist tour operator for single people.

Age groups   28 – 55 yrs
             45 – 69 yrs

0207 951 2822

Solo's Holidays
ATOL 0559

I

The Plough Inn
LONGPARISH

The Place For
Seafood, Game & Steak Specialities
- Extensive Range of Fresh Fish Daily
- Fine Wines & Real Ales
- Bar Food Menu

MOST CREDIT CARDS ACCEPTED

J

Fantastic Reader Offers
UP TO 40% OFF

THE LAND'S END Hotel

DINNER B&B

Fr only **£34.50** pppn
(min 2 nights, 2 adults share)

Land's End Hotel and its fabulous new Longships Restaurant with breathtaking views across The Atlantic Ocean ...
... offers Comfort with Luxury

CALL NOW FOR FANTASTIC FESTIVE BREAKS

For further Information & Reservations
CALL: 01736 871955
Land's End Hotel, Sennen, Cornwall, TR19 7AA
OFFERS SUBJECT TO AVAILABILITY

K

5 STAR EDINBURGH
★★★★★ AT ★★★★★
FRINGE PRICES

£300 PER COUPLE buys 2 nights of weekend luxury in the heart of one of Europe's most beautiful capitals. Including full Scottish breakfast plus dinner with wine on one night, in the hotel's stylish Terrace Restaurant.

L

ST. JAMES' BRASSERIE

A WIDE CHOICE OF EXQUISITE DISHES
& WINES FOR THE CONNOISSEUR

Dine at our 13th. Century Inn
The perfect venue for the perfect evening

OPENING HOURS MON-SAT FROM 6 PM
SUNDAY FROM 12 NOON

01222 87537

RUDRY, CAERPHILLY CF83 3EA

2 Language Elements – Part 1

Read the following letter and decide for items 21–30 which word a, b, or c is missing. Mark your answers on the answer sheet.

Dear David,

Thank you very much for your letter, _____²¹ I received last week. Sorry I haven't replied sooner but I _____²² very busy looking for a job at the moment.

I was pleased to hear that you are enjoying your new job. It _____²³ be very nice for you to be earning some money after all _____²⁴ years studying! How do you like living in London? Very exciting, I'm sure.

I've got an interview next week for a job in sales. I _____²⁵ to an advertisement in the paper last week and then received a phone call _____²⁶ the Sales Manager. The job _____²⁷ very interesting and the salary is quite good. I'll let you know if I'm _____²⁸.

Maybe we can get together some time in the next few weeks. I could _____²⁹ come to London one weekend. It _____³⁰ be nice to see you again and I might have some good news about my interview.

Best regards,
John

21	a what b which c who	**24**	a these b this c those	**27**	a hears b listens c sounds	**30**	a could b should c would
22	a am b was c will be	**25**	a answered b replied c telephoned	**28**	a succeeding b success c successful		
23	a might b must c would	**26**	a from b to c with	**29**	a easier b easily c easy		

Mock Exam Tasks

2 Language Elements – Part 2

Read the following fax and decide which word a–o is missing in items 31–40. Mark your answers on the answer sheet.

FAX

Home Tuition Ltd.
F.A.O. Mr Arthur Jones
25 Oxford Road
Milton Keynes

Fax No. 01908 – 37 23 58
This page only

Dear Mr Jones

Re: Your advertisement in 'The Daily Telegraph' of 20 March

I am writing in _____ 31 to your advertisement for 'host families' and would like to apply as a future 'family'. I feel that our home might be _____ 32 for your foreign students. We have two spare rooms which are both very clean and _____ 33, each with a private bathroom. Both rooms are big enough for a desk.

Our house is not far _____ 34 the city centre. The main shops, cinema, theatre, and leisure centre are only a few minutes' walk away. We are also very _____ 35 to the beach which might be nice for students to visit in the summer.

My wife is a very good cook and she wouldn't mind _____ 36 all the meals. We would also be very happy to _____ 37 our guests to our friends and neighbours. I am sure they would _____ 38 meeting foreign students and it would be good practice for the students!

If you _____ 39 any further information or if you would like to come and visit us at home, please feel free to contact me. I am also sending a few pictures of the house, the rooms and the garden.

I look _____ 40 to hearing from you soon.

Yours sincerely

Matthew Saunders

a chance	b close	c comfortable	d enjoy	e forward
f from	g holiday	h introduce	i make	j need
k providing	l response	m suitable	n visit	o would

47 Mock Exam Tasks

3 Listening Comprehension – Part 1: Listening for Gist

You are going to hear five people talking about food.
You will hear each statement only once.

*After you have listened to a person's statement, decide what the opinion of that person is and mark on the answer sheet **true** (+) or **not true** (-).*

Now you will have about one minute to read the five sentences.

41 The first speaker believes that milk is not the same product as it used to be.

42 The second speaker thinks that people want the same quality of food all year round.

43 The third speaker does not want to pay more for healthy, natural food.

44 The fourth speaker feels that cooking and eating habits have stayed the same.

45 The fifth speaker thinks that good food also costs more.

3 Listening Comprehensions – Part 2: Listening for Detail

You are going to hear a conversation between a Radio 2 reporter and Quentin Cooper, a technology expert, on the way people use computers these days.

First, read the sentences below. You will have two minutes for this. Then listen to the conversation. While you listen, mark whether the sentences are true (+) or not true (-) on the answer sheet. After that, you will hear the conversation again.

Now read the sentences 46 to 55.

46 According to the report, quite a lot of pensioners spend more than ten hours a week using a computer.

47 Quentin Cooper's father does not know how to use a computer.

48 According to the report, computers are the most popular thing to talk about for one in ten families in Britain.

49 The reporter thinks that everything we write in the future will be on the computer.

50 Cooper thinks that computers will stop people from reading and writing.

51 Quentin Cooper thinks that somebody has to make sure that only good and useful information is on the Internet.

52 40% of homes in Britain now have a computer.

53 According to Quentin Cooper, it is not necessary for everybody to have the possibility of using a computer.

54 Quentin Cooper thinks that everybody will have a computer by 2005.

55 Quentin Cooper says that people will stop using libraries in the future.

3 Listening Comprehension – Part 3: Selective Listening

*You will hear five short texts. Read the questions, listen to the text, and then decide whether the answer is **yes** (+) or **no** (-) and mark the correct box on your answer sheet.*
You will hear each text twice.

56   You are phoning your English friend, Graham Bennet, to arrange to meet him tomorrow, Tuesday, 25th, and hear the following message on his answering machine.

      Can you meet Graham tomorrow?

57   You are on holiday in the South of England. You are listening to the weather report because you and your friends want to go walking tomorrow.

      Will the weather be suitable for walking tomorrow?

58   You want to take a bus from Bristol to Gatwick Airport on Sunday morning.

      Can you take a bus at 6 am on Sunday?

59   You ring British Airways to change your flight reservation.

      You need to press '2'.

60   You are going to spend a few days in London this week and ring the London Tourist Board.

      To find out what's on this week you will have to ring 0839123-400.

Mock Exam Tasks

4 Letter Writing

The English Language Holiday Club

Practise and improve your English while visiting some of Britain's most beautiful scenery.
Guided walks in small groups according to age, interests and fitness!
Unique 'walk and talk' English training. All guides are qualified and experienced English teachers.
Write today for a membership application form and further information.
Please enclose some brief personal details.
Please write to:
E.L.H.C.
P.O. Box 27
Torquay
TQ2 5AY

You decide to write for more information. Write the letter using a suitable greeting and a suitable closing formula. The following four points should be mentioned in your letter.

Before starting the letter decide the order in which you think these points should be included.

- Three items of information about yourself
- Ask for more details (eg cost, dates, size of groups)
- Reason for your letter
- Why you are interested in their offer

Mock Exam Tasks

Answer Key

1 Reading Comprehension – Part 1: Reading for Gist
- 1 G
- 2 H
- 3 J
- 4 A
- 5 I

1 Reading Comprehension – Part 2: Reading for Detail, Text 1
- 6 b
- 7 c
- 8 a

1 Reading Comprehension – Part 2: Reading for Detail, Text 2
- 9 c
- 10 a

1 Reading Comprehension – Part 3: Selective Reading
- 11 G
- 12 A
- 13 F
- 14 H
- 15 B
- 16 J
- 17 E
- 18 I
- 19 L
- 20 D

2 Language Elements – Part 1
- 21 b
- 22 a
- 23 b
- 24 c
- 25 b
- 26 a
- 27 c
- 28 c
- 29 b
- 30 c

2 Language Elements – Part 2
- 31 l
- 32 m
- 33 c
- 34 f
- 35 b
- 36 k
- 37 h
- 38 d
- 39 j
- 40 e

3 Listening Comprehension – Part 1: Listening for Gist
- 41 T
- 42 T
- 43 NT
- 44 NT
- 45 T

Answer Key

3 Listening Comprehension – Part 2: Listening for Detail

46 T
47 NT
48 T
49 T
50 NT
51 NT
52 NT
53 T
54 NT
55 NT

3 Listening Comprehension – Part 3: Selective Listening

56 N
57 Y
58 N
59 N
60 Y

Script Listening Comprehension – Part 1: Listening for Gist

41 Very few people know what a natural product should actually look and taste like. The milk I buy, for example, has changed. It looks thinner, it looks whiter and it seems to me it tastes sweeter. I'm afraid in ten or fifteen years' time I won't recognize milk any more when I pick it up off the counter. I think it's becoming a prepared food.

42 I think it's the consumers who are partly responsible. They expect consistent food, no matter what the nature of the food. They want the same size, the same shape, the same colour all year round. They don't want to find insects in their salads or worms in their apples. So they get what they want.

43 It certainly seems to me that there is a move towards much healthier eating generally. I am quite concerned about where my food comes from, particularly organic foods. And I'm prepared to spend a little more. The only question is: how can I be certain that the more expensive food from the market or the supermarket is really natural and untreated?

44 We live in a fast world. People do not seem to have time for the most basic things in life. A lot of people don't want to spend time in their kitchen in the evening preparing a good, wholesome meal for the family. They'd rather buy mass-produced, ready-made food (fast-food), which takes ten minutes to heat in the microwave and which they can eat in front of the telly.

45 Good food costs a lot to produce. It's not cheap to make in any way. One thing we the British, as a nation, have to learn is to be prepared to pay a little more for our food. If we don't want to spend money on food, if we want cheap food, we will get cheap quality. If we want quality food, we have to pay more for it.

Script Listening Comprehension – Part 2: Listening for Detail

Reporter According to a survey out today, British people are turning off their TVs and turning to computers and amongst the keenest computer users these days are the so-called 'Silver Surfers', the over sixties who are spending more than ten hours a week at their keyboards. Quentin Cooper, what about the 'Silver Surfers'? Isn't there a certain misunderstanding that computers are for young people and not for older ones?

Cooper Oh, yes. First, there is the idea that computers-for-fun are for young people. The second idea is that computers-for-work are for all people. Nobody seems to think of older people. My dad in particular – he's well past retirement age – he started tentatively doing a little bit of word processing and writing the odd letter and now he's designing Christmas cards and labels on his computer. He's getting a whole lot out of it.

Reporter From your experience, do you know of people who say, "When we get home in the evening we don't actually sit and watch the telly, we actually go and surf the net"?

Cooper Well, one of the things this survey has shown is that in ten per cent of households, computers are the main family conversation subject of the week. Now, I find that rather alarming.

Reporter What about people who say, "This is the end of the world as we know it. People are going to stop talking to each other"? Certainly, when it comes to handwriting, I can see handwriting being obsolete in thirty years' time, and that the whole fabric of society will change as a consequence.

Cooper I think we are still going to need to write notes. Computers in some ways actually encourage people to read because whether it is a game or whether it is an encyclopaedia, you're going out there and you're finding information. It encourages people to use their brains. Like with all these things they can be used wrongly. You can spend all your time on the Internet going to porn sites or you can spend all your time on the internet doing something useful. It's the same with TV, the same with radio. The problem isn't the medium, it's what you do with it.

Reporter Is there a real problem, though, that the people who have computers are going to be one step ahead of the rest of the country who don't?

Cooper We still only have one in four households in Britain with a computer and I don't think everybody needs a computer. I know it's not my job as a technology person to say this, but it's right for some people – and not right for others.

Reporter When is more than half the population going to have to have a computer?

Cooper Very soon. I think we're talking about by something like the year two thousand and five. It may not be that everybody uses the computer a lot. It'll be like a library: some people will go in there all the time, some people will go in there a bit. The key lesson that people are learning is as with a library you don't feel guilty about all those sections of the library you don't go to. You just go to the bits that you want. People started off with computers feeling terrible about the fact that computers could do all these things and they weren't using them properly. Now people are beginning to understand: customize the computer to suit your life; don't customize your life to suit the computer.

Mock Exam Tasks

Script Listening Comprehension – Part 3: Selective Listening

56 Hello, this is Graham Bennett on eight-two-double-eight-three-oh. Sorry, I'm not able to speak to you directly at the moment. I'm away on business for a few days and will be back in my office on Thursday, the twenty-seventh. But please leave a message after the tone or speak to my assistant Christina by dialling 'nought'. Thank you.

57 Tonight for the whole of the United Kingdom it'll turn quite chilly. Apart from some showers for parts of Scotland, it'll be dry. Zero to four degrees for England and Wales, zero to minus two for Scotland and Northern Ireland, the lowest for tonight. Tomorrow, it'll be much drier and brighter, especially in the south. On Monday, we'll start to see more rain arrive.

58 Hello, this is National Express Talking Timetables for the following route: Bristol to Gatwick Airport. Coaches leave from the bus station in Bristol. Unless otherwise stated, times apply seven days a week. The first one leaves Bristol at 6 am and arrives at Gatwick at 8.45 am – this bus does not run on Sundays. Then times are as follows: 7.30 am arrives 10.05; 9 am arrives 11.20; 10.30 am arrives 1 pm.

59 Welcome to British Airways. Please choose one of the following four options: if you're a member of our Executive Club, please press 'one', if you would like to make a reservation, please press 'two', if you already have a reservation and wish to confirm or change it, press 'three'. Finally, for any other general enquiry please press 'four'. Alternatively, please stay on the line and you will be connected to one of our representatives.

60 Hello, this is the London Tourist Board. You will now hear a list of the phone services we provide. All numbers begin oh-eight-three-nine-one-two-three followed by three numbers for the specific topic. We'll start with current events. For what's on this week dial oh-eight-three-nine-one-two-three followed by four-hundred. Main events in the next three months are on four-oh-one. A special service providing details of events for children is on four-oh-four.